UK price
£6.95

A HANDBOOK OF
POPULAR
HOUSEPLANTS

Peter Chapman • William Davidson • Margaret Martin

a Salamander book

Published by Salamander Books Limited
LONDON • NEW YORK

A SALAMANDER BOOK

Published by Salamander Books Ltd.,
129/137 York Way,
London N7 9LG,
United Kingdom.

© Salamander Books Ltd. 1990

ISBN 0 86101 498 7

Distributed by Hodder and Stoughton Services,
PO Box 6, Mill Road, Dunton Green,
Sevenoaks, Kent TN13 2XX

CREDITS

Introduction written by: David Squire
Editor: Geoff Rogers
Assistant Editor: Lisa Dyer
Designer: Kathy Gummer
Line artwork: Tyler/Camoccio Design Consultants and Maureen Holt
Filmset: SX Composing Ltd., Essex, England
Colour separation: Scantrans Pte Ltd., Singapore

Printed in Belgium by Proost International Book Production

PICTURE CREDITS

The majority of the photographs in this book were
taken by Eric Crichton. Other photographs are credited
as follows on the page: (T) Top, (B) Bottom.

Peter Chapman & Margaret Martin: 24(T), 40(T)
Frans Noltee: 31(B)
Harry Smith Photographic Collection: 31(T), 44(B)
Michael Warren: 38

Right: *These mini cyclamen show
their beautiful pastel shades and
shuttlecock-shaped petals.*

INTRODUCTION

Houseplants are indispensible, turning a house into a home and creating colour and interest throughout the year. This book offers an exciting array of plants, from those with exquisite flowers to others which are grown for their handsome and unusually-shaped leaves. Also included are palms and ferns with their attractive foliage and dignified appearance, as well as bromeliads and cacti.

The plants in this lavishly illustrated book have been selected to enable you to decorate your home with confidence. Some of these plants are relatively short-lived, creating a burst of colour at one particular time, while others are known for their longevity and ability to become permanent ornamental features. There are houseplants available in almost every shape and size imaginable. Some are small enough to decorate windowsills and coffee-tables, while others eventually dominate a corner or alcove. In short, there are plants for every room in the house and to suit all tastes.

Using this book

The plants are arranged in alphabetical order according to their scientific (botanical) names. Unfortunately, botanists sometimes have second thoughts about a plant and give it a new name but the old name frequently remains in popular use. Each plant in this book has been given the name by which it is usually sold. If it has an alternative scientific name, this will also be indicated, as well as any common names. Common names are important to most plant enthusiasts,. not only because they are the most familiar names but also because they can be amusing and descriptive.

The keys to success with houseplants are usually simple and easily achieved. Highlighted under each plant name is quick reference information to assure the most favourable conditions for cultivation. This includes light, water, feeding and temperature requirements. Plants needing *cool* conditions should have winter temperatures of 13-18°C (55-65°F); for *intermediate* conditions, maintain a temperature of 18-24°C (65-75°F) and for *warm* conditions, 24-27°C (75-80°F).

Each entry includes a description of the plant and often some of its varieties. Specific information on composts, disease, general care and propagation is also included to help you get the most from your houseplants.

Selecting plants for the home

When buying a houseplant, never accept one that is weak and unhealthy, as it will not recover and give you the long-term pleasure of a well-grown plant. There is always the temptation to buy an inexpensive plant, but if it lives for only a week it can be a very costly buy. Reject plants that are spindly or infested with pests and diseases. The plant should be labelled and the compost neither waterlogged nor bone-dry. If roots are emerging out of the drainage hole in the pot, the plant needs to be repotted and is short of food. In winter, do not buy plants which have been left outside to be chilled by cold winds, while in summer avoid those which are wilting and in strong sunlight. Always insist that the plant is wrapped or put in a paper-sleeve to ensure that it reaches home safely.

Adiantum capillus-veneris
(Dudder grass, Maidenhair fern, Venus's-hair fern)

► **Light shade**
► **Temp: 18-21°C (65-70°F)**
► **Moist surroundings**

This is one of the most delicate and beautiful foliage plants with pale green fronds which contrast with the black stems.

Bright, direct sunlight and dry atmospheric conditions will prove fatal. Offer maidenhair ferns lightly shaded positions in a warm room: place plants in a large container and surround their pots with a moisture-retaining material such as peat. Misting of foliage is often recommended, but this exercise can have undesirable effects if the surrounding air temperature is low. It is therefore better to use the mister to wet the soil surface.

Avoid the use of chemicals on foliage. When potting on, a peaty mixture is needed and, once plants have been established in their pots, weak liquid feeding will be needed every time the plant is watered. During the winter months, feeding is not important and watering should be only sufficient to keep the soil moist.

Take care
Slugs find this foliage desirable.

Aechmea fasciata
(Exotic brush, Silver vase, Urn plant, Vase plant)

► **Intermediate conditions**
► **For everyone**
► **Easy to bloom**

The most popular plant of the bromeliad group, *Aechmea fasciata* grows to 75cm (30in) with wide leathery leaves of green and frosty white. Tufted blue and pink flower heads appear in spring and last until summer, or even longer. Plants are compact, vase-shaped and beautiful.

Grow the urn plant in bright indirect light in 7.5-10cm (3-4in) pots filled with medium-size fir bark. Water moderately all year but keep 'vase' of plant filled with water at all times, except when the temperature falls below 13°C (55°F). Mist foliage occasionally. Plants are almost pest-free – the leaves are too tough.

Start new plants from rooted offshoots. When they are 7.5-10cm (3-4in) high, cut them off and pot in individual containers of bark.

Take care
Only feed with a weak solution – in summer only.

Above left: Adiantums come in many varieties, most with beautiful, delicate foliage which must be protected from bright sunlight.

Above: Aglaonema commutatum 'Pseudobracteatum' is an interesting subject for adding height and colour to indoor collections.

Left: Perhaps the most popular bromeliad, Aechmea fasciata has silver-banded green leaves and a beautiful, tufted inflorescence. It will bloom readily and the colour lasts for months.

Aglaonema commutatum 'Pseudobracteatum'

(Golden evergreen)
► Light shade
► Temp: 18-21°C (65-70°F)
► Keep moist

A demanding plant and best suited to the experienced grower. The principal difficulty is the high temperature, which must be maintained. A height of 100cm (40in) is not unusual in mature specimens. Leaf perimeter is green with a centre of whitish yellow.

New plants are propagated from top sections of stems with three sound leaves attached. Severed ends are allowed to dry for a few hours before being treated with rooting powder. Plant in peaty mixture in small pots and plunge in moist peat in a heated propagating case. To ensure success, the temperature should be around 21°C (70°F). When potting cuttings for growing on, put three cuttings in a 13cm (5in) pot, using a potting mixture with a percentage of loam.

Mealy bugs are sometimes found where the leaf stalks curl round the main stem. In this situation, thorough saturation with liquid insecticide will be needed.

Take care
Ensure adequate temperature.

Alocasia indica

(Elephant's-ear plant)
► Light shade
► Temp: 18-24°C (65-75°F)
► Keep moist

Alocasia indica is one of the more exotic and temperamental members of the Araceae family. There are numerous cultivars, all with exotic velvety appearance and arrow-shaped leaves.

Their most important needs are for a temperature of around 24°C (75°F) and for a humid atmosphere. The soil in the pot must be kept moist at all times and it is essential that the surrounding atmosphere is also moist. This will mean placing the plant on a large tray filled with gravel, which should be kept permanently wet. The tray can contain water, but the level should never be up to the surface of the pebbles so that the plant pot is actually standing in water. Plants allowed to stand in water become waterlogged and will rot and die. Feeding is not important, but it will do no harm if liquid fertilizer is given periodically.

Take care
Keep plants out of draughts and away from hot radiators.

9

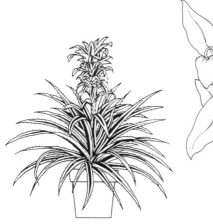

Ananas bracteatus striatus

(Ivory pineapple, Red pineapple)
► **Good light**
► **Temp: 13-18°C (55-65°F)**
► **Keep on dry side**

The best of the South American bromeliads, the green form of which, *A. comosus*, is the pineapple of commerce. A white variegated form of *A. comosus* is also known as the ivory pineapple.

In good light, the natural cream colouring of the foliage will be a much better colour, but one should avoid very strong sunlight that is magnified by clear glass. Wet root conditions that offer little drying out will also be harmful. Feed occasionally but avoid overdoing it. New plants can be produced by pulling offsets from mature plants and potting them individually in a mixture containing leaf-mould and peat. In reasonable conditions, plants can be expected to develop small pineapples in about three years. Although highly decorative, these pineapples tend to be woody and inedible. However, as they are developing, the central part around the base of the leaves will change to a brilliant reddish pink.

Take care
Avoid the spined leaf margins.

Anthurium scherzerianum

(Flamingo flower, Pigtail plant, Tailflower)
► **Light shade**
► **Temp: 16-21°C (60-70°F)**
► **Keep moist and fed**

This is a small relative of *A. andreanum*. It is well suited to average room conditions, in both space requirements and care. Green leaves are produced on short stems from soil level, and flowers are generally red in colour and produced over a long spring and summer period. The spadix in the centre of the flower has a whorl to it that gives rise to one of its common names, pigtail plant.

All anthuriums require an open potting mixture, and one made up of equal parts of peat and well-rotted leaves will be better than an entirely peat mix or a mix containing loam. Once established, plants need regular feeding to maintain leaf colouring and to encourage production of flowers with stouter stems – weak-stemmed flowers need support. Keep this plant out of bright and direct sunlight.

Take care
Provide humid conditions.

bove: Anthurium scherzerianum appears almost artificial. The brilliant red spathes of anthuriums appear over the spring and summer months. Regular feeding maintains the leaf colouring.

Above: An Ardisia crenata covered with red berries makes a fine winter gift. Leaves are dark green and handsome. This plant from the East Indies looks attractive when set in window gardens.

eft: An extremely ornamental member of the bromeliad family, Ananas bracteatus striatus will develop dazzling colour in good ight. However, avoid very strong sunlight, especially in summer.

Above: Aralia elegantissima is a striking plant with very dark green, almost black, foliage which is delicate on young plants but becomes coarse with age. Older plants also lose their lower leaves.

Aralia elegantissima
(Dizygotheca elegantissima)
(False aralia)

▶ **Light shade**
▶ **Temp: 18-21°C (65-70°F)**
▶ **Keep moist**

Increasingly this is sold as *Dizygotheca elegantissima* and is one of the most attractive of the purely foliage plants. It has dark green, almost black, colouring to its leaves. Graceful leaves radiate from stiff, upright stems that will attain a height of about 300cm (120in). As the plant ages, it loses its delicate foliage and produces leaves that are much larger and coarser in appearance. One can remove the upper section of stem and new growth will revert to the original delicate appearance.

Warm conditions with no drop in temperature are important. Water thoroughly, soaking the soil and allow to dry reasonably before repeating. Feed in spring and summer, less in winter.

Mealy bug can be treated with a liquid insecticide. Affected areas should be thoroughly saturated with the spray. Root mealy bugs can be seen as a whitish powder. To clear, water in insecticide.

Take care
Avoid fluctuating temperatures.

Ardisia crenata
(Ardisia crispa)
(Coral berry, Spiceberry)

▶ **Light shade**
▶ **Temp: 16-21°C (60-70°F)**
▶ **Keep moist and fed**

Although flowers are produced, the main attractions of the coral berry are the glossy-green, crenellated leaves and the long-lasting berries. It grows very slowly and plants take several years to attain the maximum height of around 90cm (36in). A stiff, upright central stem carries the wood branches.

Offer a lightly shaded location for best results, and at no time be tempted to water excessively. Slow growing plants of this kind are best kept on the dry side, particularly in winter. It is important to feed only lightly and to discontinue feeding altogether in winter. Plants with a slow growth rate are better grown in pots that are on the small side. Soil with a good percentage of loam must be used, as plants will quickly deteriorate in peat mixtures.

Cuttings of firm young shoots can be taken in spring and rooted in peat at not less than 21°C (70°F) to produce new plants.

Take care
Never overwater in winter.

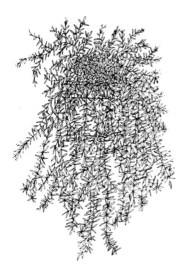

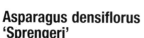

Asparagus densiflorus 'Sprengeri'

(Asparagus fern, Emerald feather, Emerald fern)
▶ **Good light, no sun**
▶ **Temp: 13-18°C (55-65°F)**
▶ **Water and feed well**

Though the common names suggest a fern, this is a member of the lily family. One of the most vigorous and useful of all the many fine foliage plants, it is especially effective in a hanging basket.

New plants can be raised from seed sown in spring or one can divide mature plants at almost any time of year. Before division, ensure that the soil is thoroughly wetted. As with potting on, divided pieces should be planted in pots that give the roots space. The potting mixture must contain a reasonable amount of loam. In order to keep the lush green colouring, it is important that well-rooted plants should be fed regularly. Feeding with weak liquid fertilizer at every watering is often more satisfactory than giving plants occasional heavy doses. Although plants will appreciate good light, it is important to protect them from direct sun.

Take care
Avoid cold winter locations.

Aspidistra elatior

(Bar-room plant, Cast iron plant, Iron plant)
▶ **Light shade**
▶ **Temp: 13-18°C (55-65°F)**
▶ **Keep moist**

The *Aspidistra elatior* has been popular since Victorian times, when it acquired its common names on account of its ability to withstand trying conditions. The aspidistra has been around for a very long time and there are plants alive today with a known history that goes back for over a century. Although a tough plant, the aspidistra will only just survive in a spartan environment. However, if agreeable conditions are provided, the plant will flourish.

Reasonable light, evenly moist conditions that avoid extremes, and occasional feeding once the plant is established, will usually produce plants that are fresh and lush. When potting on, use a properly prepared mixture of soil that contains a good percentage of loam. Any good fertilizer will suit well-rooted plants.

There is a very attractive variegated form with striped green and white leaves.

Take care
Never use chemicals on foliage.

Above: *Aspidistra elatior is a tough plant that can withstand poor light, a smoky atmosphere and low temperatures. However, it flourishes when given healthy conditions.*

Above right: *Smooth, pale green leaves radiate from the centre of Asplenium nidus avis. This plant needs moist conditions.*

Right: *Here is a plant that can brighten any autumn day. Azalea indica is a compact shrub that can be in flower for many weeks.*

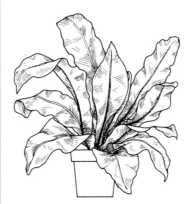

Asplenium nidus avis
(Bird's nest fern, Nest fern)

▶ **Shade**
▶ **Temp: 18-24°C (65-75°F)**
▶ **Moist roots and surroundings**

As small plants, these are not very exciting, but once they have been advanced to pot sizes of around 18cm (7in) they have few equals. Growing these plants to perfection is difficult. Surrounding objects touching tender leaves will almost certainly cause damage, as will spraying with unsuitable chemicals or the presence of slugs.

Leaves can be kept in good order if a temperature of around 21°C (70°F) is maintained and plants enjoy good light but not direct sun. Open, peaty mixture is needed when potting, and water applied to the top of the soil should immediately flow through. Frequent feeding of established plants with weak fertilizier is preferred to infrequent heavier doses. Keep the soil moist.

Scale insects can be seen as dark brown or flesh-coloured spots adhering to the area around the midrib of the leaf. These can be sponged off.

Take care
Never handle young foliage.

Azalea indica
(Rhododendron simsii)
(Indian azalea)

▶ **Cool conditions**
▶ **For a challenge**
▶ **Difficult to bloom**

A fine small-leaved evergreen shrub, *Azalea indica* makes a handsome plant with brilliant white, pink, red or purple flowers from midsummer to winter. The plant will eventually grow to about 75cm (30in) – a handsome accent for cool indoor gardens.

Grow this plant at a bright window – sun is not necessary. Use a rich potting soil of equal parts of humus and standard houseplant mix. Water heavily most of the year with lime-free water but, after bloom, taper off moisture and keep the soil just barely moist. Cut back to 10-15cm (4-6in) and resume watering when growth starts. Feed every 2 weeks during growth but not at all the rest of the year.

Azaleas require the coolest place at your window and need frequent misting to keep humidity high (about 40 per cent).

Take care
Never allow soil to dry out. Put plant outside in a cool, moist place through the warm summer months.

13

Begonia masoniana

(Iron cross begonia)

▶ **Light shade**
▶ **Temp: 16-21°C (60-70°F)**
▶ **Keep dry in winter**

This fine plant grows to splendid size if given reasonable care. The rough-surfaced leaves are a brownish green and have a very distinctive cross that covers the greater part of the centre of the leaf and radiates from the area where the petiole is joined. This marking resembles the German Iron Cross.

During the spring and summer months, it will be found that plants grow at reasonable pace if given a warm room, moist root conditions and weak liquid fertilizer with each watering. Plants that have filled their existing pots with roots can be potted on at any time during the summer, using a loam-based potting mixture and shallow pots. Over the winter months, loss of some lower leaves will be almost inevitable but, provided the soil is kept on the dry side during this time, the plant will remain in better condition and will grow with fresh leaves in spring.

Take care
Inspect for winter rot.

Begonia rex

(King begonia, Painted-leaf begonia, Rex begonia)

▶ **Light shade**
▶ **Temp: 16-21°C (60-70°F)**
▶ **Keep on the dry side in winter**

These rank among the finest foliage plants, with all shades of colouring and intricate leaf patterns. Those with smaller leaves are generally easier to care for.

To propagate, firm mature leaves are removed from the plant and most of the leaf stalk is removed before a series of cuts are made through the thick veins on the underside of the leaf. The leaf is then placed underside down on moist peat (in either boxes or shallow pans) and a few pebbles are placed on top of the leaf, to keep it in contact with the moist peat. Temperatures in the region of 21°C (70°F) are required, and a propagating case. Alternatively, the leaf can be cut into squares of about 5cm (2in) and the pieces placed on moist peat.

When purchased, these plants are often in pots that are much too small. Repot the plant into a larger container without delay.

Take care
In humid conditions, look out for signs of mildew.

Above: *Distinctive brown marking in the centre of the leaf give Begonia masoniana the apt common name of iron cross begonia. These rough textured plants will develop into neat, rounded shapes as they age.*

Left: *A wealth of colour in the foliage and intricate leaf patterns place the Begonia rex among the elite of houseplants. Small-leaved types are often easier to raise.*

Right: *Bougainvillea is a popular red or purple flowering plant, perfect for the sunny window. With careful culture, it will bloom freely throughout the summer.*

Bougainvillea
(Paper flower)

▶ **Warm conditions**
▶ **For a challenge**
▶ **Difficult to bloom**

Bougainvillea indoors? Why not. This climbing plant bears handsome red or purple bracts in midsummer (the flowers are insignificant) and needs space, for it grows to 180cm (72in) or more if conditions are suitable. It responds well to pruning to size, however, this should be done immediately after flowering. The leaves are mid or dark green in colour.

Grow bougainvillea at the sunniest window you have and use a rich potting soil. Add one cup of humus to a 20cm (8in) pot. Plants are greedy and need plenty of water and feeding every 2 weeks while in active growth. However, do not feed in cool weather when the plant slows down; also water sparingly then. The plants should be rested throughout the winter.

Be alert for red spider, which occasionally attacks plants – use a suitable chemical preventative or mist thoroughly to discourage infestation. Grow new plants from stem cuttings.

Take care
Bright sunshine is essential.

Caladium hybrids
(Angels' wings, Elephant's-ear, Fancy-leaved caladium, Mother-in-law plant)

▶ **Light shade**
▶ **Temp: 18-24°C (65-75°F)**
▶ **Keep moist when in leaf**

There is a wide variety of these hybrids, all in need of some cosseting if they are to succeed. Adequate temperature is essential, but these plants are sensitive to the effects of bright sun through clear glass.

When potting, it is important to use a high proportion of peat that will drain freely. Repot over-wintered tubers soon after they have produced their first new growth. Old soil should be teased gently away, care being taken not to damage any new roots that may be forming. Rather than transfer plants to very large pots, it is better, having removed much of the old soil, to repot into the same container using fresh soil.

Leaves of these plants will not tolerate any cleaning. When buying plants, get them from a reliable retailer with heated premises, as cold conditions for only a short time can be fatal.

Take care
Provide adequate storage warmth.

Calathea makoyana

(Brain plant, Cathedral windows, Peacock plant)

▶ **Shade**
▶ **Temp: 18-24°C (65-75°F)**
▶ **Keep moist and fed**

Oval-shaped, paper-thin leaves are carried on leaf-stalks that may be as much as 60cm (24in) long and are intricately patterned. The peacock plant is of a delicate nature; it will rapidly succumb if the temperature is not to its liking. And it must at no time be exposed to direct sunlight or shrivelling of leaves will occur.

Small plants are seldom offered for sale. It is usual for the specialist grower to raise plants in very warm beds of peat in the greenhouse. When plants are well established, they are potted up into 18cm (7in) pots. For all potting operations, a very peaty and open mixture containing some coarse leaf-mould will be essential. And following potting, it will be necessary to ensure that the soil remains just moist but never becomes saturated for long periods.

Established plants have to be fed with weak liquid fertilizer weekly from spring to autumn.

Take care
Protect form direct sunlight.

Calceolaria hybrids

(Lady's pocketbook, Lady's slippers, Pocketbook plant, Pouch flower, Slipper flower, Slipperwort)

▶ **Cool conditions**
▶ **For everyone**
▶ **Easy to bloom**

Though the flowering period is relatively short – only a few months – these colourful 25cm (10in) high plants are popular and add a note of festivity to a house. Many hybrids are available in a variety of stunning colours from dark yellow to brilliant reds.

Grow at a sunny but cool window in a rich soil. Keep moderately moist at all times. Do not feed. Sow seeds in spring or summer for new plants. Try to maintain cool temperatures – 13°C (55°F) for best growing. These hybrids will not succeed in heat. When the flowering period is over, discard plants.

Take care
Do not keep the compost excessively wet, as the roots will quickly rot.

Above: Calceolaria hybrids are annual garden plants but they are frequently grown indoors for their abundance of slipper-shaped, highly coloured flowers.

Right: A natural trailing plant, Ceropegia woodii has grey-coloured, heart-shaped leaves that have a succulent, puffed up appearance.

Ceropegia woodii

(Hearts entangled, Hearts
on a string, Rosary vine,
String of hearts)

▶ **Suspend in good light**
▶ **Temp: 13-18°C (55-65°F)**
▶ **Moist, but dry in winter**

With the current fashion for
hanging plants of all kinds, this is
the ideal plant to try, as it is so
different from almost all other
potted plants. Small, fleshy, heart-
shaped leaves are attached to wiry
stems that hang perpendicularly
from the plant. *C. woodii* is a
hanging plant with no desire
whatsoever to climb or do anything
different. The leaves are mottled
and grey-green in colour and the
flowers are pink and tubular.

The common name of hearts
entangled comes from the manner
in which the foliage twines around
itself when the plants are growing
actively. There is also the
additional fascination of the
gnarled bulbous growths that
appear at soil level and along the
stems of the plant, from which new
growth sprouts. Indeed, the bulbils
with growth attached can be used
to propagate fresh plants or they
can be raised from cuttings.

Take care
Avoid overwet winter conditions.

Chamaedorea elegans

(Neanthe bella)

(Good luck palm, Parlour palm)

▶ **Light shade**
▶ **Temp: 16-21°C (60-70°F)**
▶ **Keep moist but well-drained**

For people with limited space who
wish to grow a palm, this is the
answer, as the parlour palm
presents a neat and compact plant
throughout its life.

This plant is often used in bottle
gardens, where it takes place of
honour as the taller plant to give
the miniature garden some height.
One might add a word here to say
that, when planting bottle gardens,
it is most essential to ensure that
small, non-invasive plants are
selected.

The parlour palm should not be
allowed to dry out excessively,
although it should be a little on the
dry side during the winter months
when growth is less active. It is
important to ensure that the pot is
well-drained, and this will mean
putting a layer of broken pieces of
clay pot in the bottom of the new
container before adding soil. Water
poured onto the surface of the soil
should be seen to flow fairly
rapidly down through the mixture.

Take care
Avoid using chemicals on leaves.

Chlorophytum comosum 'Variegatum'

(Ribbon plant, St. Bernard's lily, Spider ivy, Spider plant, Walking anthericum)

▶ Airy, good light
▶ Temp: 10-16°C (50-60°F)
▶ Frequent feeding

The chlorophytums of the houseplant world appear to be everywhere. Yet they are not always as bright and healthy as their ease of culture would suggest they should be. This may be due to the fact that owners feel that they are so easy to grow that they don't have to bother at all.

Given the chlorophytum good light to prevent it becoming thin and straggly. Keep it moist at all times, especially during summer.

The most important need of all, and the one most neglected, is that of feeding, and feeding the spider plant means giving it very much more than the average indoor plant. Frequent potting on is also essential. This could be necessary twice a year for vigorous plants. Spider plants produce large fleshy roots and quickly become starved if not given sufficient nourishment.

Take care
Aphids cause blotched leaves.

Chrysanthemum

(Florist's mum, Pot chrysanthemum)

▶ Cool conditions
▶ For beginners
▶ Easy to bloom

Potted chrysanthemums of yellow, bronze, white or red make beautiful plants indoors. There are many hybrids of these plants that make fine temporary seasonal plants for the home. The most popular types are the dwarf chrysanthemums that reach 15-25cm (6-10in) and can flower during any season.

Grow chrysanthemums at a bright but not sunny window. Keep them as cool as possible: 16°C (60°F) is ideal. Use a rich soil and keep quite moist throughout blooming.

After flowering, plants are best discarded. If plants are kept, they will not produce a display the following year, as they have been grown under special light and temperature regimes, and may have been treated with chemicals to keep them dwarf-size.

Take care
Keep plants well-watered, especially when they are flowering.

Above: Chrysanthemums grown in pots for decoration indoors will last up to six weeks. They are good value-for-money plants and are available in many colours such as bronze, yellow, white or red.

Above: Chlorophytum comosum 'Variegatum', the familiar spider plant or spider ivy, develops masses of natural plantlets at the end of long stems. These can be used for propagating new plants.

Right: Cineraria is one of the finest gift plants. This well-known favourite has daisy-like flowers in a spectrum of brilliant colours. It is well worth growing from seed if you want a challenge. Keep this plant cool until buds form.

Cineraria cruenta
(Senecio cruentus)
(Cineraria)

► **Cool conditions**
► **For a challenge**
► **Difficult to bloom**

Although now botanically known as *Senecio cruentus*, it is invariably sold as *Cineraria cruenta*. They are attractive plants with flowers in vibrant shades of red, blue and purple. Each plant comes into flower from December to June, remaining in flower for about three weeks. After flowers fade, they must be discarded. However, they are worth their price for providing a stunning seasonal display.

Keep plants at a bright but not sunny window and soil should be watered evenly at all times. To keep plants blooming, maintain cool temperatures of about 13-16°C (55-60°F). Sun and warmth will desiccate cinerarias. Be careful of the cineraria mite, which is prevalent on plants – use any of the suitable pesticides with caution.

Take care
Grow in coolness – 7-10°C (45-50°F) – until buds form.

Cissus antarctica
(Kangaroo vine)

► **Light shade**
► **Temp: 13-18°C (55-65°F)**
► **Keep moist**

As the common name suggests, these plants originate from Australia. The mid green leaves have toothed margins and are seen at their best when plants are allowed to climb against a framework or wall. In favourable conditions, stems will add metres (yards) of growth, but trimming back to shape can be undertaken at any time of year, so there is no possibility of them out-growing their welcome. These are useful plants for the more difficult and darker indoor location.

Cuttings consisting of two firm leaves with a piece of main stem attached will root at any time if a temperature of around 18-21°C (65-70°F) can be maintained. Treat cuttings with a rooting powder. It is advisable to put several cuttings in one pot when they are removed from the propagator.

Peat compost will suit them fine, but it is essential that feeding is not neglected when plants are growing in this sort of mixture.

Take care
Dry soil will cause leaf loss.

Right: *Columnea banksii variegata is an eye-catching trailing plant with small green and white leaves. Ideal for hanging baskets.*

Far right: *This earth star, Cryptanthus bromelioides tricolour, has an extended growth habit and beautiful year-round colour.*

Below right: *Cyclamen persicum is a stately and delicately flowered plant which blooms in autumn and winter. Cyclamen grow wild along the eastern Mediterranean shores.*

Below: *This variety is Codiaeum 'Eugene Drapps' and is by far the best yellow-coloured of the commonly named Joseph's coat plants. As for all codiaeums, watch for red spider mite.*

Codiaeum hybrids

(Croton, Joseph's coat, Variegated laurel)

▶ **Good light**
▶ **Temp: 16-21°C (60-70°F)**
▶ **Feed and water well**

Best known as crotons, these codiaeums are among the most colourful of all foliage plants, as the common name Joseph's coat suggests. A particularly beautiful form called 'Eugene Drapps' has yellow, lance-shaped leaves.

Full light, with protection from the strongest sunlight, is essential if plants are to retain their health and bright colouring. There is also a need for reasonable temperature, without which shedding of lower leaves will be inevitable. Healthy plants that are producing new leaves will need to be kept moist with regular watering, but it is important that the soil should be well-drained. Frequent feeding is necessary, though less is needed in winter. Large plants that seem out of proportion to their pots should be inspected in spring and summer. If well-rooted, they should be potted into large pots using loam-based compost.

Take care
Check regularly for red spider.

Columnea banksii variegata

(Variegated goldfish plant)

▶ **Light shade**
▶ **Temp: 16-21°C (60-70°F)**
▶ **Keep moist in summer**

The columneas are generally free-flowering plants, but the variegated form of *C. banksii* can be included among foliage plants, as it rarely produces flowers. The foliage is highly variegated, slow growing, and pendulous. The leaves are plump and fleshy, and attached to slender dropping stems. Plants are seen at their best when suspended in a basket or hanging pot.

Cuttings are more difficult to root than the green forms of columnea. Short sections of stem with the lower leaves removed are best for propagating. Treat with rooting powder before the cuttings, five to seven in small pots, are inserted in a peat and sand mixture. A temperature of at least 21°C (70°F) is necessary and a propagator will be a great advantage. Due to the very slow rate of growth, it is necessary to allow the soil to dry reasonably between waterings. Feed with weak fertilizer, but never overdo it.

Take care
Keep reasonably warm.

Cryptanthus bromelioides tricolor

(Earth star, Pink cryptanthus, Rainbow-star)
▶ Light shade
▶ Temp: 16-21°C (60-70°F)
▶ Keep on dry side

The pink, green and white colouring of this plant can be spectacular in well-grown specimens, but they are not easy plants to care for. Although grouped with the other flatter-growing cryptanthuses under the same common name of earth star, these have a slightly different habit of growth. The centre of the plant tends to extend upwards, and new plant growth sprouts from the side of the parent rosette. If these side growths are left attached to the parent, a full and handsome plant will in time develop. They can also be removed when of reasonable size by pulling them sideways. It is then simple to press the pieces into peaty mixture for them to produce roots.

Almost all cryptanthuses are terrestrial and are seen at their best when nestled in the crevices of an old tree stump or surrounded by a few stones.

Take care
Avoid wet and cold conditions.

Cyclamen persicum

(Alpine violet, Sowbread)
▶ Cool conditions
▶ For a challenge
▶ Difficult to bloom

Grown from a tuber, this is a charming plant up to 40cm (16in) tall, with flowers in red, pink or white. The pretty heart-shaped leaves are dark green or silver. Single, double or fringed flowers start appearing in late winter.

Keep the cyclamen out of direct sun. Start the tubers, one to a 13cm (5in) pot, in late summer in a rich potting mix of equal parts of humus and soil. Set the top of the tuber slightly above the soil surface; otherwise, water may collect in the crown and cause rot. Keep the soil moist and the plants in coolness at 13-16°C (55-60°F). Feed every 2 weeks while in growth. When flowers fade in early spring, let the plants rest by gradually withholding water until the foliage dies. Keep nearly dry with the pot on its side in a shady place in coolness, until autumn. Then remove dead foliage and repot in fresh soil mix.

Take care
Give plenty of water. Keep cool and humid (but do not spray the flowers). Give a resting period.

Cyperus alternifolius
(Umbrella palm, Umbrella plant, Umbrella sedge)

▶ Light shade
▶ Temp: 13-18°C (55-65°F)
▶ Wet conditions

This is an ideal plant for houseplant enthusiasts who excessively water indoor plants. It loves to have its roots constantly in water. The narrow, green leaves have little attraction, but green flowers produced on stems that may attain 75cm (30in) have a certain fascination.

When grown indoors, these water-loving plants must be given all the water they require. Although it would be death to most houseplants, place the pot in a large saucer capable of holding a reasonable amount of water. Ensure that the water level is regularly topped up.

Established plants will benefit from regular feeding, given from spring to late summer.

Take care
Keep permanently wet.

Dieffenbachia maculata 'Exotica'

(Dumb cane, Mother-in-law's tongue plant, Spotted dieffenbachia, Tuftroot)

▶ Light shade
▶ Temp: 16-21°C (60-70°F)
▶ Keep moist and fed

During recent years, many new varieties of dieffenbachias have become available. Many are forms of *Dieffenbachia maculata*. 'Exotica' is a very colourful and attractive variety, usually growing to about 60cm (24in) high and creating a superb plant for decorating rooms indoors. It has a tough constitution, tolerates low temperatures, and, if not too wet, does not seem to suffer. It produces clusters of young plants at the base of the parent stem and can be propagated easily by removing the basal shoots and planting them separately in small pots filled with peat. Once rooted, they should be potted in a peaty houseplant compost. Shoots can often be removed with roots attached, but protective gloves should be worn.

Take care
Never get sap on to your skin or in your eyes.

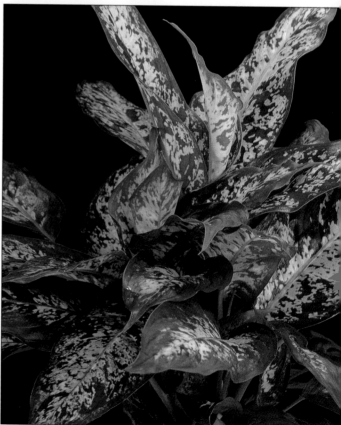

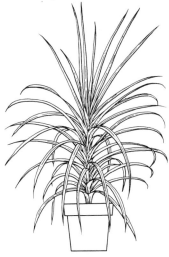

'Bausei'

Dracaena deremensis

(Striped dracaena)

▶ **Light**
▶ **Temp: 16-21°C (60-70°F)**
▶ **Keep on the dry side**

There are numerous improved forms of this dracaena, all erect with broad, pointed leaves up to 60cm (24in) long. The variations are mostly in leaf colour: *D. deremensis* 'Bausei' has a dark green margin and glistening white centre; in *D. deremensis* 'Souvenir de Schriever' the top-most rosette of leaves is bright yellow, but the leaves revert to the grey-green with white stripes of the parent plant as they age.

An unfortunate aspect of this type of dracaena is that they shed lower leaves as they increase in height, so that they take on a palm-like appearance with tufts of leaves at the top of otherwise bare stems. Although loss of lower leaves is a natural process, the incidence of dying and falling leaves will be aggravated by excessive watering. Water thoroughly, and then allow the soil to dry reasonably before repeating. These are hungry plants and will be in need of regular feeding.

Take care
Never allow to become too wet.

Dracaena marginata tricolor

(Madagascar dragon tree, Variegated silhouette plant)

▶ **Good light**
▶ **Temp: 16-21°C (60-70°F)**
▶ **Avoid wet conditions**

This plant has a natural tendency to shed lower leaves as it increases in height. Nevertheless, it can be an elegant plant if carefully grown, having attractive light and darker colouring running along the entire length of the slender, pointed leaves.

The main stem of the plant will need a supporting cane to remain upright. Plants sometimes produce young shoots naturally along the main stem so that multi-headed plants result. Alternatively, one can remove the growing tip of the main stem when the plant is about 60cm (24in) tall, so that branching is encouraged. If plants are grown in wet soil, they may suffer from leaf damage. The soil for these plants should always be on the dry side, especially during winter.

Feeding is not desperately important, but weak liquid fertilizer during the spring and summer months will do no harm.

Take care
Keep warm, light and dry.

23

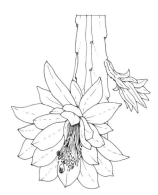

Echeveria derenbergii

(Baby echeveria, Painted lady)

▶ **Full sun**
▶ **Temp: 4-30°C (40-85°F)**
▶ **Keep moist all year**

Echeveria derenbergii is a charming small plant that does equally well in the greenhouse or on a sunny windowsill. It is a small, tightly leaved rosette, which forms offsets to make a small cushion. The bluish-grey leaves end in a red tip. The plant flowers freely during summer. The petals of the small bell-shaped flowers are yellow inside and orange outside.

Echeverias are easy to cultivate, in a loam- or peat-based medium, with moderate watering in summer and a dose of high-potassium fertilizer every two weeks. In winter, keep slightly moist. In the wild, echeverias shed their lower leaves during the winter dry period, as a way of conserving moisture. In cultivation, even though the plant is not short of water, the lower leaves still shrivel, leaving a rather untidy plant in the spring. Remove the offsets and restart the plants in early spring.

Take care
Do not let water collect in the centre of the rosette.

Epiphyllum 'Ackermannii'

(Orchid cactus)

▶ **Partial shade**
▶ **Temp: 4-27°C (40-80°F)**
▶ **Keep almost dry in winter**

Epiphyllums are among the most un-cactus-like cacti and are often grown by plant lovers who profess no interest in conventional cacti. Nevertheless, they are true cacti, but live naturally in tropical rain-forests rather than in the desert. Plants normally cultivated are hybrids between the various wild species and other cacti. Such plants are hardier and have more colourful flowers. 'Ackermannii' is a typical example and is one of the oldest in cultivation, but its flowers have not been surpassed in beauty of colour. They are about 8cm (3.2in) across and brilliant red but not perfumed. The flower blooms appear along the notched edges of the stems and they may last for several days.

You can grow epiphyllums in a standard houseplant mixture, but if you add extra peat or leaf-mould to it, this is beneficial. Also, good drainage is important.

Take care
Feed with high-potassium fertilizer when in bud and flower.

Far left: *Echeveria derenbergii is one of the most beautiful of the echeverias and one of the easiest to grow. The brightly coloured flowers are carried on short stems.*

Left: *The stems of Euphorbia milii are covered in sharp prickles. Bright red bracts give this shrub great appeal. Avoid exposure to cold draughts in winter.*

Below: *The popular Euphorbia pulcherrima shows mid-winter colour with large showy bracts in red, pink or white. Here, several individual plants are grouped together; each produces bracts of a single colour.*

Euphorbia milii
(Euphorbia splendens)
(Christ plant, Christ thorn, Crown of thorns)

▶ **Intermediate conditions**
▶ **For everyone**
▶ **Easy to bloom**

Well known and well liked, this 75cm (30in) plant with dark green leaves bears small vivid red bracts surrounding insignificant flowers in winter. The stems have prickles, but the plant is very amenable to indoor culture and worth its space.

Grow the crown of thorns in a bright sunny window. Pot in equal parts of standard houseplant soil and sand that is kept evenly moist all year except in winter and early spring, when a slight drying out is beneficial. Feed monthly in summer and autumn, but not at all the rest of the year. Plants resent drafts but like good air circulation. Take new plants from cuttings during the spring.

This plant will exude a poisonous sap from cut surfaces, so handle with gloves.

Take care
Ensure that this plant has a slight rest after blooming has finished.

Euphorbia pulcherrima
(Christmas flower, Christmas star, Lobster plant, Mexican flame leaf, Painted leaf, Poinsettia)

▶ **Intermediate conditions**
▶ **For a challenge**
▶ **Difficult to bloom**

This highly prized indoor plant grows up to 75cm (30in). Leaves are scalloped and mossy-green. The 'flowers' are leafy bracts turning fiery red, white or pink.

The poinsettia needs a bright but not sunny location and intermediate temperatures about 18°C (65°F) or a little above. Grow in a rich, porous houseplant soil. Drainage must be perfect. In winter, when the plant is in bloom, keep soil evenly moist. Reduce moisture when the leaves start to fall and keep the plant cool.

In spring, put the plant in the garden but leave it in its pot. Cut back and replace in fresh soil. In late summer, bring the plant back into the house. In autumn, provide a period of uninterrupted darkness – at least 14 hours a day – to initiate flower buds for the winter.

This plant is poisonous and should be handled with gloves.

Take care
Avoid drafts and keep the compost evenly moist.

25

Fatshedera lizei

(Aralia ivy, Botanical-wonder tree, Ivy tree, Tree ivy)

▶ Light shade
▶ Temp: 4-16°C (40-60°F)
▶ Keep moist and fed

This plant does not have the flexibility of the stems of Hedera (ivy) which is one of its parents, but is more in keeping with the stems of Fatsia which is the other parent. Leaves have the shape of the ivy leaf and are glossy-green in colour. For cooler locations, the ivy tree is ideal, as it prefers low rather than high temperatures and is hardy in sheltered areas. Plants have a tendency to lose lower leaves, especially in hot, dry conditions.

New plants may be propagated either from the topmost section of the plant with three firm leaves attached or from sections of stem with a single leaf attached. In both cases they will do well in a temperature of around 18°C (65°F) if inserted in peat and sand mixture. In order to provide plants of full appearance, it is best to put three or four rooted cuttings in the growing pot rather than one. The soil for potting up cuttings should be on the peaty side.

Take care
Avoid hot conditions.

Ficus benjamina

(Benjamin tree, Java fig, Small-leaved rubber plant, Tropic laurel, Weeping fig)

▶ Good light, no direct sun
▶ Temp: 16-21°C (60-70°F)
▶ Keep moist and fed

Of very graceful weeping habit, F. benjamina will develop into tree size if provided with the right conditions. However, excess growth can be trimmed out at any time. To maintain plants in good condition with their glossy leaves gleaming, it is important to feed them well while in active growth and to pot them on into loam-based mixture as required. Little feeding and no potting should be done in winter. It is also wise during this period to water more sparingly unless the plants are drying out in hot rooms. The weeping fig has a tendency to shed leaves in poorly lit situations.

As well as the normal all-green leaved type, there are varieties with variegated leaves. Additionally, some varieties have delicately cut leaves.

Take care
Avoid placing in dark areas.

Above: The naturally glossy green leaves of Fatshedera lizei are attached to strong stems that will eventually need some support.

Above right: One of the symbols of the houseplant business, the rubber plant, Ficus robusta, has broad glossy-green leaves and stout upright stems. It is ideal for filling a large corner.

Left: The elegant Ficus benjamina has glossy foliage and naturally cascading branches – a combination that produces one of the finest foliage plants.

Right: The silvery-grey colouring of Fittonia verschaffeltii 'Argyroneura Nana' is heavily veined with a tracery of darker green that gives the oval leaves an attractive appearance. This plant has a creeping nature.

Ficus robusta
(Assam rubber tree, India rubber tree, Rubber plant)
▶ **Light shade**
▶ **Temp: 10-18°C (50-65°F)**
▶ **Avoid very wet conditions**

Often the symbol of the modern-day houseplant business, the rubber plant is still grown and sold in large quantities. *Ficus robusta* now seems firmly established as the favourite rubber plant and we seldom see its predecessors these days. The original variety was *F. elastica*, which in time was replaced by *F. decora*. The new plant is superior in almost every way, particularly in its ability to stand up to indoor conditions.

Failure with these plants usually arises from overwatering. Permanently wet soil results in roots rotting away, which will mean loss of leaves. It is especially important to prevent plants becoming too wet during the winter months. During the winter, it is also wise to discontinue feeding. Potting should be undertaken during late spring or early summer, using loam-based mixture. Leaves will be brighter if occasionally cleaned with a damp sponge.

Take care
Protect from sun through glass.

Fittonia verschaffeltii 'Argyroneura Nana'
(Silver-net plant, Little snakeskin plant, Mosaic plant)
▶ **Shade**
▶ **Temp: 18-24°C (65-75°F)**
▶ **Keep moist and humid**

This smaller-leaved version of the silver snakeskin plant is much less demanding than its big brother, *Fittonia verschaffeltii*. The leaves are oval and produced in great quantity. Neat growth and prostrate habit makes them ideal for growing in bottle gardens or disused fish tanks.

Cuttings root with little difficulty in warm, moist and shaded conditions. Several cuttings should go into small pots filled with peaty mixture, and it is often better to overwinter these small plants rather than try to persevere with larger plants. At all stages of potting on a peaty mixture will be essential. It is better to use shallow containers that will suit the plant's prostrate growth.

Not much troubled by pests, the worst enemy is low temperature allied to wet root conditions. Recommended temperature levels must be maintained.

Take care
Avoid wet and cold combination.

Grevillea robusta

(Silk oak, Silky oak)

► **Light shade**
► **Temp: 4-21°C (40-70°F)**
► **Feed and water well**

An Australian plant, the silk or silky oak makes a splendid tree in its native land and is a fairly fast-growing pot plant in many other parts of the world. It is tough, has attractive, green silky foliage and is one of the easiest plants to care for. *Grevillea robusta* can be readily raised from seed.

The grevillea will quickly grow into a large plant if it is kept moist and well fed, and if it is potted into a larger container when the existing one is well filled with roots. A loam-based soil is best. If plants become too tall for their allotted space, it is no trouble to remove the more invasive branches with a pair of secateurs – almost any time of the year will do for this exercise.

During the summer months when the plant is in full vigour, it will be important to ensure that it is obtaining sufficient water. This will mean filling the top of the pot and ensuring that the surplus runs right through and out at the bottom drainage holes.

Take care
Water well in summer.

Hedera canariensis

(Algerian ivy, Canary Island ivy, Madeira ivy)

► **Good light**
► **Temp: 4-16°C (40-60°F)**
► **Keep moist and fed in summer**

This is one of the most rewarding indoor plants of them all, having bright green and white variegation. It is undemanding to grow and will climb or trail. The principal need is for light, cool conditions and a watering programme that allows for some drying out of the soil between soakings.

In hot, dry conditions, plants may become infested with red spider mite. These are minute insects that increase at an alarming rate if left to their own devices. In time, the mites will make tiny webs from one part of the plant to another, but initially they are difficult to detect and are almost invariably found on the undersides of leaves. When infested with mite, the leaves tend to curl inwards and appear hard and dry. Thorough and frequent drenching with insecticide is the best cure and should be done carefully out of doors on a still day.

Take care
Avoid hot, dry conditions.

Far left: When well grown, the leaves of Grevillea robusta have a silvery sheen that is most attractive. These vigorous plants need frequent feeding.

Left: The unusual warm golden-yellow colouring places this ivy, Hedera helix 'Goldchild', ahead of most foliage plants.

Below left: Hedera canariensis needs good light to maintain its colourfully variegated foliage. In poor light, the foliage colour will revert to green.

Below: Depending on variety, Hibiscus rosa-sinensis produces large, showy flowers in red, orange, pink, yellow or white. Grows and blooms outdoors as well as indoors. Sun is essential.

Hedera helix 'Goldchild'
(Golden English ivy)

▶ **Good light**
▶ **Temp: 7-16°C (45-60°F)**
▶ **Keep moist and fed**

There is a wide range of ivies, many with small and variegated leaves. All are ideal for growing as houseplants but this is one of the loveliest ivies of them all, having green and gold foliage with gold being much more predominant. Shallow plastic saucers for larger flower pots are excellent for displaying them in. Saucers should have holes made in their base, and several young plants are then planted in the containers. The result will be a flat mass of golden greenery.

Cool, light conditions are best and will help considerably in reducing the incidence of red spider mite. Smaller-leaved ivies develop a black rot among their stems and foliage if they are allowed to become too wet and the conditions are dank and airless. When watering, give a thorough application and then allow to dry reasonably before repeating. Feed in spring and summer.

Take care
Avoid hot and dry conditions.

Hibiscus rosa-sinensis
(Blacking plant, China rose, Chinese hibiscus, Rose of China)

▶ **Warm conditions**
▶ **For everyone**
▶ **Easy to bloom**

A large 120cm (48in) free-flowering plant, hibiscus grows well in tubs in a porch or garden room. Plants have lush green foliage and bear mammoth, paper-thin, red, pink, orange, white or yellow flowers that each last only a few days, followed by more flowers. Bloom continues for about six weeks in midsummer.

Sun is the key to success with hibiscus, so put them at the sunniest window. Grow in equal parts of soil and sand, and be sure drainage is perfect. Flood with water during growth, for these are thirsty plants. Feed every two weeks. Spray foliage with tepid water. Prune back small specimens to 10cm (4in) in early spring, large plants by one third. Watch for spider mites, which like these plants. Propagate by taking cuttings in spring.

Take care
Keep out of drafts and fluctuating temperatures, as these may cause the buds to drop.

Hippeastrum hybrids
(Amaryllis, Barbados lily)

▶ **Intermediate conditions**
▶ **For beginners**
▶ **Easy to bloom**

These striking bulbous plants with strap foliage bear large flowers in many colours. The stalks are up to 65cm (26in) long. Plants make a colourful display in early spring.

Buy good quality bulbs in autumn and start in growth during the winter. Use one bulb to a 15-18cm (6-7in) clay pot. Allow 2.5cm (1in) space between the walls and the bulb. Let the upper third of the bulb extend above the soil line. Use any standard houseplant soil. Set the pot in a cool, shady place and grow almost dry until the flower bud is 15cm (6in) tall. Then move the pot into a sunny window and water heavily.

After the plant blooms, keep it growing so the leaves can make food for next year's flowers. When foliage browns, let the soil go dry for about 10 to 12 weeks or until you see new flower buds emerging. Then replant in fresh soil. Propagate by seeds or by removing offsets when repotting.

Take care
Continue to feed until all the leaves have died down.

Howeia forsteriana
(Kentia forsteriana)
(Forster sentry palm, Kentia palm, Paradise palm, Sentry palm, Thatch-leaf palm)

▶ **Light shade**
▶ **Temp: 16-21°C (60-70°F)**
▶ **Water and feed well in summer**

Howeia forsteriana is one of the most elegant and interesting of all the plants grown in pots for indoor decoration, but it is tending to become increasingly expensive. Also known as *Kentia forsteriana* – most of the seed for growing these plants commercially still comes from their natural home of Lord Howe Island in the South Pacific.

All palms need an open, fibrous, potting mixture. It is wise to put a layer of clay pot shards in the bottom of the container.

The long upright leaves of these plants are sensitive to many of the chemicals used for controlling pests and for cleaning foliage, so it is wise to test any products on a small section of the plant. Wait for a week to see the reaction. Do not expose plants to full sun or to cold conditions following any application of chemicals.

Take care
Avoid wet winter conditions.

Above: The large-flowered Hippeastrum hybrids are glorious bulbs which can be brought into bloom every year with a little care. Keep them slightly potbound and repot every three or four years.

Above right: Hoya bella has small dark green leaves and waxy clusters of fragrant white-purple flowers that perfume a room. This fine plant is especially rewarding in an indoor hanging basket.

Left: The elegant Howeia forsteriana provides an ideal, decorative plant for the home. Proceed with caution if using any chemical treatments.

Right: The flowers are the chief attraction of this little succulent, Huernia zebrina. They are large for such a small plant and most strange in appearance, with a slightly unpleasant smell.

Hoya bella
(Miniature wax plant)

▶ **Intermediate conditions**
▶ **For a challenge**
▶ **Difficult to bloom**

This 30-60cm (12-24in) vining plant resembles its larger cousin *Hoya carnosa*. This plant is excellent for small window gardens and hanging baskets. Leaves are small and dark green and the plant has waxy, purple-centered, white fragrant blooms.

Grow the miniature wax plant in bright light. Use a well-drained potting soil of equal parts of humus and houseplant soil. Grow in small pots for best results. Give plenty of water in spring, summer, and autumn. In winter let the soil go almost dry. Feed monthly during warm weather. Mist the foliage frequently and check for mealy bugs, which adore wax plants. Do not remove stems on which flowers have been produced; they are also the source of next season's bloom. Propagate by cuttings in spring.

Take care
Do not disturb the plant after the buds form, as this encourages them to fall off.

Huernia zebrina
(Little owl eyes, Owl eyes)

▶ **Full sun**
▶ **Temp: 4-30°C (40-85°F)**
▶ **Keep almost dry in winter**

The name refers to the zebra-like stripes on the flowers of this miniature succulent – if a zebra could have purple-brown stripes on a yellow background! But, accurate or not, this flower is delightfully attractive and unusual. The five striped lobes surround a thick purple central ring, the whole flower being about 4cm (1.6in) across. There is almost no smell, but what there is is unpleasant and characteristic of most of the stapelia-type succulents! The plant itself consists of sharply toothed, angled stems, bright green and 8cm (3.2in) long.

Grow this huernia in a mixture of two parts of a standard material and one part of sharp sand or perlite. Never allow the potting mixture to become too wet, or rot or infection can set in. This is indicated by black marks or black tips to the stems. In winter, give only enough water to prevent severe shrivelling, but in spring and summer water freely.

Take care
Treat black marks with fungicide.

Hyacinthus orientalis
(Dutch hyacinth, Hyacinth)

▶ **Cool conditions**
▶ **For beginners**
▶ **Easy to bloom**

Erect bulbous plants with 25cm
(10in) stems, hyacinths have long
narrow leaves. Flower spikes are
closely packed with waxy, very
fragrant flowers available in shades
of red, blue, yellow and white. This
plant can be forced to bloom in
spring or winter, but only once –
then they should be planted
outside. Many varieties are
available.

Grow at a bright window – sun is
not necessary. Use a potting mix
of equal parts of soil and humus
that drains readily. Water freely
when the plant is growing. Be
careful to keep cool at 10°C (50°F)
and in a dark place until growth is
under way, then bring out into the
light. Rest for 8 weeks after
flowering. Leave the plant in the
pot in a cool place. Do not feed.
Grow new plants from offsets. It
can also be grown over water.

Take care
High temperatures when the bulbs
are flowering soon cause them to
deteriorate.

Hypoestes sanguinolenta
(Freckle face, Measles plant, Pink
dot plant, Polka dot plant)

▶ **Good light**
▶ **Temp: 10-16°C (50-60°F)**
▶ **Keep moist and fed**

In the last few years, the
hypoestes has enjoyed a new
lease of life through the
introduction of a much more
colourful cultivar with a greater
proportion of pink in its leaves.

Plants are easy to manage,
although they frequently suffer
through being confined to pots too
small for the amount of growth that
these quick growers will normally
produce. Any purchased plant that
appears to be in too small a pot
should be potted into a larger one
without delay. Use loam-based
potting soil, as peat mixtures can
be fatal for this plant if they dry out
excessively. Also, it is wise to
remove the growing tips so that
plants branch and become more
attractive. Untidy or overgrown
stems can be removed at any time,
and firm pieces about 10cm (4in)
long can be used for propagation.
Extremely dry soil will cause loss
of lower leaves, so check daily to
ensure that the soil is moist.

Take care
Avoid drying out of soil.

Above: The scarlet-veined leaves of Iresine herbstii give the plant an unparalleled brilliance. To keep the vivid colour, give plenty of light, but avoid the noonday sun.

Far left: The polka dot plant, Hypoestes sanguinolenta, forms a beautiful picture of delicate, pink-mottled leaves. Untidy plants can easily be pruned and the trimmings used as cuttings.

Left: Jasminum polyanthum is a splendid climbing plant from China with fragrant white and pale pink flowers. It needs support to be displayed to best advantage.

Iresine herbstii

(Beef plant, Beefsteak plant, Blood leaf, Chicken-gizzard)

▶ **Good light**
▶ **Temp: 13-18°C (55-65°F)**
▶ **Keep fed and watered**

These fall among the cheap and cheerful range of plants and have foliage of a very deep, almost unnatural, red. Cuttings root very easily and plants are quick to grow. They can be propagated successfully on the windowsill if shaded from direct sun.

Mature plants, however, must have a very light place if they are to retain their colouring, and will only need protection from strong midday sun. During the spring and summer, plants must be kept active by regular feeding and ensuring that the soil does not dry out excessively. When potting on becomes necessary, a loam-based mixture should be used. Plants will soon use the nourishment in peat mixes even if fed regularly. At all stages of growth, the appearance of the plant will be improved if the tips are periodically removed.

Besides the red-coloured variety, there is *I. herbstii aureoreticulata*, which is yellow.

Take care
Feed well in summer.

Jasminum polyanthum

(Pink jasmine)

▶ **Intermediate conditions**
▶ **For everyone**
▶ **Easy to bloom**

This beautifully fragrant jasmine has mid green leaves and white and pale pink flowers from autumn to spring. Plants climb to 300cm (120in) or more and need support. This is a good offbeat plant for the indoor garden.

Grow jasmine in sun – otherwise it will not do well and will not flower. Use a rich potting mix of equal parts humus and soil. Feed with acid fertilizer every month during growth. Mist foliage occasionally and give pots a deep soaking in the sink once a month. Provide ample humidity (50 per cent). Repot every second year. Propagate new plants from cuttings in spring.

Take care
Provide ample sun and very good ventilation. Keep cooler in winter at 13°C (55°F) during flowering.

Kalanchoe blossfeldiana
(Flaming Katy)

▶ **Intermediate conditions**
▶ **For beginners**
▶ **Easy to bloom**

This 30cm (12in) succulent has leathery green leaves and bright red flowers in winter, making it especially appealing. Bloom sometimes occurs again in spring. Hybrids are available with pink, white or yellow flowers.

Grow at a bright window, but exercise caution because sunlight can scorch this plant. Use a standard houseplant soil – add one cup of sand to a 15cm (6in) pot. Do not feed. Allow soil to dry out between waterings. Do not mist plants, as the succulent leaves will be harmed. Any water on the base of the plant or foliage can cause rot. Provide good ventilation. Trim back bottom leaves when they become too thick. Repot every second year. Propagate new plants from seed in spring or stem cuttings in summer.

Take care
Do not overwater at any time, but especially not in winter.

Maranta leuconeura 'Erythrophylla'
(Herringbone plant, Prayer plant, Ten-commandments)

▶ **Light shade**
▶ **Temp: 18-24°C (65-75°F)**
▶ **Moist soil and atmosphere**

With reddish-brown colouring and intricately patterned, rounded leaves, this is one of the more attractive smaller plants. Exotic colouring immediately suggests that it is difficult, but the reverse is true if sufficient warmth is maintained and care given.

These plants are best grown naturally with foliage trailing where it will. Unless the leaves are misted twice daily, hanging containers will usually prove to be too dry a location for them. It will be better to grow plants at a lower level. To improve humidity around the plant, place the pot in a larger container with moist peat packed between the two pots.

Peaty mixture is essential when potting on, but one should not be too hasty in transferring plants to very large pots. Fertilizer should be very weak and given to the plant with each watering rather than in a few heavy doses.

Take care
Avoid bright sunlight.

Above: Kalanchoe blossfeldiana produces masses of brilliant flowers from autumn to spring. It is well-known as a houseplant and easy to restart from cuttings.

Above right: The interesting leaves of Monstera deliciosa are perforated in older plants and are deeply cut along their margins. Strong aerial roots are produced from the stem.

Right: With reddish-brown and green coloured, intricately marked leaves, Maranta leuconeura 'Erythrophylla' is a very colourful foliage plant.

Mimosa pudica

(Action plant, Humble plant,
Live-and-Die, Sensitive plant,
Shame plant, Touch-me-not)

▶ **Light shade**
▶ **Temp: 16-21°C (60-70°F)**
▶ **Keep moist and fed**

These are attractive little plants
with fern-like foliage. They are
grown as annuals, fresh seed
being sown each spring and old
plants discarded at the end of the
summer. The main attraction of
this particular plant lies in its habit
of collapsing completely during the
day when the foliage is touched. In
time, the plant becomes erect
again, but it is an eerie sight.

These plants are frequently
offered for sale in very small pots
that have little nutrient left in the
soil. These should be potted into
standard houseplant mixture as
soon as possible.

Actively growing plants should
be kept moist and fed regularly.
Freshly potted plants should be
allowed to establish in new soil
before being fed. A position in light
shade is suggested.

New plants may be raised from
spring-sown seed or from cuttings
of older plants taken in autumn.

Take care
Pot on to avoid starvation.

Monstera deliciosa

(Breadfruit vine, Fruit-salad plant,
Hurricane plant, Mexican
breadfruit, Split-leaf philodendron,
Swiss cheese plant, Window plant)

▶ **Light shade**
▶ **Temp: 16-21°C (60-70°F)**
▶ **Moist roots, regular feeding**

The naturally glossy-green leaves
with attractive deep serrations
make the monsteras among the
most popular of all indoor foliage
plants. The aerial roots produced
from the stems of more mature
plants are an interesting and often
perplexing feature. Removing
some excess roots will not be
harmful, but in most instances it is
better to tie the roots neatly to the
stem of the plant and to guide
them into the pot soil.

As plants mature, they will
naturally produce serrated leaves.
Darker growing conditions can
result in leaves that are smaller
and complete, rather than cut out.
Bright sunlight magnified by
window glass can cause scorching
of foliage and should be avoided,
particularly while soft new leaves
are maturing.

Take care
Avoid exposure to direct sunlight.

Neoregelia carolinae tricolor

(Blushing bromeliad, Cartwheel plant)
► **Good light**
► **Temp: 13-18°C (55-65°F)**
► **Dry at roots, urn filled**

Although it does produce small and inconspicuous flowers in the centre of the rosette of leaves (the 'urn' or 'vase'), this is very much a foliage plant. Overlapping leaves radiate from a short central trunk and are spectacularly striped in cream and green with the added attraction, as flowers appear, of the shorter central leaves and the base of larger leaves turning a brilliant shade of red.

Following this colourful display, the main rosette will naturally deteriorate and in time will have to be cut away from the small trunk to which it is attached. Take care that the small plant or plants forming around the base of the trunk are not damaged during this operation, as these will be the plants of the future. Remove young plantlets when they have developed several leaves and pot them into a peaty mixture.

Take care
Periodically change the water in the central urn of leaves.

Pandanus veitchii

(Screw pine, Veitch screw pine)
► **Good light**
► **Temp: 16-21°C (60-70°F)**
► **Avoid too wet conditions**

Of the screw pines, this is the most suitable for the average room, as it is reasonably compact and easier to accommodate. Leaves are green and white variegated and are produced in the shape of a large rosette with leaves sprouting from a stout central stem. The screw pines all have vicious spines along the margins of their leaves and a set of barbs running from the base to the tip of the leaf on the underside. Locate plants where they will be out of harm's way, perhaps by placing on a pedestal.

Being tough tropical plants that grow in exposed coastal areas, they are well adapted to harsh conditions. They will tolerate quite sunny locations and not be harmed, provided they are not too close to the window-panes. Drought conditions seem to be taken in their stride and they certainly prefer to be dry rather than too wet. Sharply draining, gritty soil is essential.

Take care
Handle plants with care.

Above: *Pandanus veitchii resembles a pineapple plant when young. Leaves radiate from a short central trunk and are white and green variegated with spined margins and undersides.*

Above: *The button fern, Pellaea rotundifolia, has very dark green, rounded leaves that form into densely foliaged plants in a comparatively short time. Needs moist and warm conditions.*

Left: *Neoregelia carolinae tricolor is a spectacular bromeliad with flat rosettes of leaves which overlap at their base to make a watertight urn. Keep this urn filled with water.*

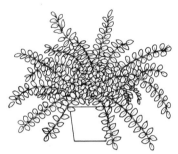

Pellaea rotundifolia
(Button fern, New Zealand cliffbrake)

▶ **Shade**
▶ **Temp: 16-21°C (60-70°F)**
▶ **Keep moist**

The button fern has dark green rounded leaves attached to firm, wiry stems, forming a dense plant.

When potting, use a peaty mixture and shallow pans. Almost all ferns in small pots will quickly become root bound and will lose their vigour if not potted on. However, inspection of roots can be misleading as these are very dark brown and the colour of the peaty soil in which they are growing, so careful inspection is needed before potting on.

Potting is best done in spring or summer and the new container should be only a little larger than the last. Roots ought to be moistened before it is removed from the pot. After potting, the soil should be well enough watered for surplus to be seen draining through the holes in the base of the pot. Then keep the newly potted plant on the dry side for several weeks – excessive drying of the mixture can be fatal.

Take care
Avoid direct sunlight.

Peperomia argyreia
(Rugby football plant, Watermelon begonia, Watermelon peperomia)

▶ **Light shade**
▶ **Temp: 13-18°C (55-65°F)**
▶ **Keep moist and fed**

This is an older plant that is not seen so frequently these days. The leaves are an interesting grey-green colour with darker stripes that radiate from the centre of the leaf. The stripes give the plant its common names.

These compact plants should be grown in shallow pans of soilless potting mixture. The location must be light, with protection from direct sunlight. Watering should be done with care; err on the side of dry rather than wet conditions. Established plants can be given weak liquid fertilizer with every watering from early spring to late summer, but none in winter. Sound leaves can be removed and cut into quarters that are placed in upright position in pure peat in warm conditions. The quartered leaf will produce roots and eventually leaves along the length of the cut edge below soil level. During propagation, ensure that cuttings do not become too wet.

Take care
Avoid winter wetness and cold.

Pereskia aculeata
(Barbados gooseberry,
Leafy cactus, Lemon vine)

▶ **Full sun**
▶ **Temp: 10-30°C (50-85°F)**
▶ **Keep slightly moist in winter**

Pereskias are the most un-cactus-like of all cacti, but their spine formation and flower structure prove their identity. This plant is scarcely succulent at all. With its large privet-like leaves and slightly spiny long trailing stems, it somewhat resembles a wild rose. The leaves are bright green, but the variety *godseffiana* has reddish tinged leaves. The stems will need supporting in some way, with sticks or a plant trellis. In a greenhouse, it can be trained up and along the roof, but the rather higher winter temperature needed makes it difficult for the cool greenhouse. Indoors, the pereskia should thrive in a light window, large enough to accommodate its trailing stems.

Pinkish flowers, rather like those of a wild rose and about 4.5cm (1.8in) across, appear in autumn, but only on large plants. Water freely in spring and summer and feed occasionally.

Take care
Cold conditions cause leaf fall.

Philodendron scandens
(Heart-leaf philodendron,
Sweetheart plant)

▶ **Shade**
▶ **Temp: 16-21°C (60-70°F)**
▶ **Keep moist and fed**

One of the smallest-leaved of all the philodendrons and possibly the best suited to the relatively smaller rooms of today. Leaves are heart-shaped and glossy green. May be encouraged to climb or trail.

Keeping the soil moist, not saturated, is important, and occasional weak feeding will suit it well. Young plants should be potted into soilless potting mixture, but older plants will respond better if potted into a mix that contains a small proportion of loam. In ideal conditions, plants may be potted at almost any time, but in the average home they will do much better if the potting can be done at the start of the summer. I am often asked for plant suggestions for dark corners and the questioner invariably wants something colourful. But such plants are few and far between; it is better to select green foliage for difficult spots, and the sweetheart plant is ideal in most cases.

Take care
Avoid dry and sunny places.

Above: Pereskia aculeata is almost like a wild rose. This is a strange non-succulent cactus which definitely needs some support.

Left: *Philodendron scandens, the sweetheart plant, has heart-shaped leaves that are deep green in colour. They will climb or trail.*

Below: *The foliage of Pilea cadierei nana is generously speckled with silver. Regular pinching out of the growing tips will produce plants of neat appearance.*

Pilea cadierei nana

(Aluminium plant,
Watermelon pilea)

▶ **Light shade**
▶ **Temp: 16-21°C (60-70°F)**
▶ **Keep moist and fed**

With silvered foliage, this is by far the most popular of the pileas, but there are numerous others, all needing similar treatment.

Plants are started from cuttings taken at any time of the year if temperatures of around 18°C (65°F) and moist, close conditions can be provided. A simple propagating case on the windowsill can offer just these conditions. Top cuttings with four to six leaves are taken, the bottom pair is removed and the end of the stem is treated with rooting powder before up to seven cuttings are inserted in each small pot filled with a peaty mixture. Once cuttings are under way, the growing tips are removed and the plants are potted into larger containers in loam-based mix.

Plants should have ample light, but should not be exposed to bright sunlight. Although small, pileas need ample feeding during the growing months if they are to retain their bright colouring.

Take care
Pinch out tips to retain shape.

Primula malacoides

(Baby primrose, Fairy primrose)

▶ **Cool conditions**
▶ **For beginners**
▶ **Easy to bloom**

With wavy edged circular leaves, this 35cm (14in) plant bears lovely pink, red, purple or white flowers in winter and spring, making it a valuable addition to the indoor garden. Generally an outdoor plant, it also does well in the home if kept really cool. Primulas have nice seasonal colour.

Select a somewhat shady place for this plant. Grow in standard houseplant soil that drains well. Keep soil moist to the touch; a dry soil will harm the plants. Feed every two weeks during the growing season. Grow cool at 10°C (50°F) if possible; warm weather can harm these plants. Occasionally this plant may be attacked by red spider, so use appropriate remedies. Get new plants by sowing seed in spring.

Take care
Keep soil quite moist during growing period. Good ventilation helps. Preferably grow in a cold frame until buds appear, then bring the plants into a cool room in the house.

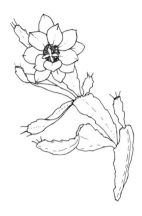

Rhipsalidopsis rosea
(Easter cactus)

► **Partial shade**
► **Temp: 10-30°C (50-86°F)**
► **Keep slightly moist all year**

This is one of the jungle cacti, related to the well-known Christmas cactus, but producing its rose-pink flowers in early spring. The flowers are about 2.5cm (1in) across. The plant itself consists of very small flattened segments, each around 2cm (0.8in) long, which, joined end to end and branching freely, eventually form a little bush. The segments carry small bushy spines along the edges and tips which are quite harmless. Propagation is simplicity itself – just remove a small branch in spring or summer and pot it up.

Although this delightful little cactus and its many hybrids can be grown as an ordinary pot plant, it is ideal for a hanging basket. Use a rich growing medium, so add about one third of peat or leaf-mould to your standard potting mixture. Give a dose of high-potassium fertilizer every two weeks in spring when buds are forming and water freely.

Take care
Spray indoor plants occasionally with clean water.

Saintpaulia ionantha
(African violet)

► **Intermediate conditions**
► **For everyone**
► **Easy to bloom**

These immensely popular gesneriads are free-flowering and dependable indoor plants.

Grow African violets at a bright but not sunny window in an area of good air circulation. A little winter sun is fine. Use standard houseplant soil that drains readily and small pots. Water the soil moderately to keep it slightly moist but never wet. Use tepid water, allowing it to stand overnight in a watering can. Feed once a month in spring, summer and autumn. Plant food rich in superphosphate will be particularly beneficial. Do not get water on the foliage as it will leave ugly marks. Dry air causes leaf curl and bud drop so maintain good humidity (but do not spray the plants). Turn the plants a quarter round monthly so that all the leaves get light. In spring propagate from leaf cuttings.

Take care
Do not pamper – allow to grow naturally. If few flowers are produced, pick them off and keep the plant on a dry regime for six weeks. This should induce bloom.

Above: *Rhipsalidopsis rosea is a cactus originating from the tropical rain forests. It needs some moisture at all times. Flowers are freely produced on flattened stem segments.*

Left: *Saintpaulia encompasses a huge group of wonderful plants with varieties in many colours. It is also available as a miniature.*

Right: *The true type of Sansevieria trifasciata 'Laurentii' has bright yellow margins to the leaves with mottled variegation in the central areas. These plants tolerate direct sunlight and can be very durable if not overwatered.*

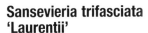

Sansevieria trifasciata 'Laurentii'

(Bowstring hemp, Devil's tongue, Good luck plant, Hemp plant, Mother-in-law's tongue)
► **Good light**
► **Temp: 16-21°C (60-70°F)**
► **Keep dry**

This plant is almost indestructible. The leaves are about 60cm (24in) long, thick and fleshy, holding a lot of moisture which the plant can draw on as needed. In view of this, it is important not to overwater.

A good watering once each month in summer should suffice, with none at all during the winter months. This may seem harsh, but if plants are to be exposed to colder winter temperatures they will get through much better if the soil in the pot is dry rather than wet. Potting ought not to be done too frequently, and one can leave the plant until it actually breaks the pot in which it is growing – the swelling bases of leaves within the pot are quite capable of breaking clay as well as plastic pots. Loam-based soil is essential when potting on. Clay pots will help to maintain the balance of these top-heavy plants.

Take care
Avoid cold and wetness together.

Schefflera arboricola variegata

(Umbrella tree, Variegated parasol plant)
► **Good light, no strong sun**
► **Temp: 16-21°C (60-70°F)**
► **Keep moist and fed**

The leaves of *Schefflera arboricola variegata* are liberally splashed with vivid yellow colouring to give the plant a glowing brightness when it is placed among others in a large display. Elegance lies in the graceful and light distribution of leaves and stems, which enables one to see through and beyond to other plants in the display. And indoors it is equally important to have graceful plants rather than a solid wall of foliage.

In common with almost all the variegated plants, this one should have a light location, but exposure to bright sun close to window-panes should be avoided if the leaves are not to be scorched. This is especially important if the leaves have been treated with chemicals. Most of the leaf-cleaning chemicals are perfectly suitable for the majority of plants, but one should never expose treated plants to direct sunlight.

Take care
Avoid winter wetness and cold.

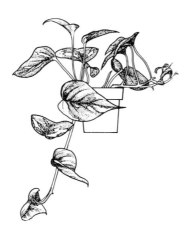

Schlumbergera × buckleyi

(Zygocactus truncatus)
(Claw cactus, Crab cactus, Linkleaf, Lobster cactus, Thanksgiving cactus)
▶ **Intermediate conditions**
▶ **For beginners**
▶ **Easy to bloom**

The crab cactus grows to about 75cm (30in) and has toothed branches that distinguish it from *Schlumbergera gaertneri*. Dozens of flowers appear in autumn and a mature plant is a fine sight. An excellent plant for hanging baskets. Many varieties are available, in different colours – red, pink, orange, and white.

Grow this jungle type cactus at a bright but not sunny window; it does not like direct sun. Use a potting mix of equal parts of medium-grade fir bark and soil. Keep plants moderately moist except in autumn, when roots should be fairly dry and plants grown quite cool at 13°C (55°F) with 12 hours of uninterrupted darkness each day for a month to encourage flower buds. Do not feed. Pieces of stem root easily in sand for new plants.

Take care
Observe period of darkness.

Scindapsus aureus

(Epipremnum pinnatum 'Aureum')
(Devil's ivy, Golden pothos, Solomon Island ivy)
▶ **Light shade**
▶ **Temp: 16-21°C (60-70°F)**
▶ **Keep moist**

This climber is best known as *Scindapsus aureus* but correctly it is now *Epipremnum pinnatum 'Aureum'*. It is an attractive plant with green, somewhat heart-shaped, leaves splashed and striped with yellow. As well as climbing, it also trails and is superb in a pot positioned at the edge of a high shelf.

Belonging to the Araceae family, it needs a reasonable amount of moisture in the pot and, if possible, also in the surrounding atmosphere. For a variegated plant, it has the truly amazing capacity of being able to retain its colouring in less well-lit places. Most other variegated plants deteriorate or turn completely green if placed in locations offering insufficient light.

Take care
Avoid hot, dry conditions.

Left: Schlumbergera × buckleyi must be the best known cactus of all and possibly also the best known houseplant. This plant should never be completely dry, although watering can be reduced after flowering.

Below left: A popular foliage plant, Scindapsus aureus can climb or trail and has lovely yellow and green variegation that is retained even in poor light.

Below: Many fine hybrids of Sinningia speciosa are available – all with the trumpet-shaped blooms in violet, red or white, some with markings in contrasting shades.

Sinningia speciosa

(Brazilian gloxinia, Gloxinia, Violet slipper gloxinia)

▶ Cool conditions
▶ For a challenge
▶ Difficult to bloom

These glamorous Brazilian plants grow up to 30cm (12in) tall and have single or double tubular flowers in vivid colours.

Gloxinias like a location where there is subdued light, so sun is not necessary to promote flowering. Grow plants in equal parts of soil and humus. Start the tubers in spring or autumn, using one to a 13cm (5in) clay pot. Set the tuber hollow side up and cover with soil (but only just). Keep evenly moist at a temperature of about 16°C (60°F).

When growth starts, increase the watering somewhat and move the plant to a slightly warmer location. When the flowers fade, gradually decrease watering, remove tops and store tubers in a dry place at 13°C (55°F). Keep soil barely moist and rest from six to eight weeks (no more) or tubers lose their vitality. Repot in fresh soil. Propagate from basal shoot cuttings, leaf cuttings or seed.

Take care
Feed weekly when buds form.

Spathiphyllum 'Mauna Loa'

(Peace lily, Spathe flower, White flag, White sails)

▶ Intermediate conditions
▶ For everyone
▶ Easy to bloom

This plant from South America has shiny green leaves and white spathe flowers that resemble anthuriums. Plants grow up to 45cm (18in) tall. In good growing conditions, this hybrid will produce fragrant flowers intermittently throughout the year. Although spathiphyllums are not showy or spectacular plants, they seem to adjust to almost any indoor location and do well.

Grow these at any exposure – they can tolerate sun or shade. Use standard houseplant soil. Allow the soil to dry out between waterings. Use a plant food about four times a year. Plants are rarely bothered by insects and seem trouble-free. For a good show, grow in 30cm (12in) pots. They make excellent room plants, even in shady corners. Propagate new plants by seed or division of the rhizomes in spring.

Take care
Keep warm and humid.

Streptocarpus hybrids
(Cape cowslip, Cape primrose)
▶ **Intermediate conditions**
▶ **For everyone**
▶ **Easy to bloom**

There is a fine new group of hybrids available that bloom almost all year, but mainly in the summer. Flower colours are white, pink or violet and the tubular flowers are indeed handsome. Plants grow to about 20-30cm (8-12in) in height and are highly recommended.

Grow the cape cowslip in a bright window, protected from direct sun. Use standard houseplant soil that drains readily. Feed every two weeks when in growth. After a bloom cycle, reduce watering; let the plant rest for about four to six weeks and then resume watering. Always use lime-free water. Do not mist the leaves; water on the foliage can cause rot. Repot annually for best results. Grow new plants from seed or leaf cuttings taken in midsummer.

Take care
Allow to rest slightly after blooming. Replace plants after two or three years as they decline in flowering vigor.

Tradescantia fluminensis 'Quicksilver'
(Wandering Jew)
▶ **Good light**
▶ **Temp: 10-16°C (50-60°F)**
▶ **Keep on the dry side**

There are numerous varieties of *T. fluminensis*, but this one is bolder and much brighter than any of the others. All, however, require very similar treatment.

Good light is important if plants are to retain their silvered variegation, but protection from bright sun will be necessary. The soil should be free to drain and at no time become waterlogged. These plants respond well to regular applications of liquid fertilizer while they are in active growth. The view that when plants are fed they tend to lose their variegation is nonsense, as variegation depends on available light and whether or not the plants are allowed to become green. In poor light, leaves tend to become green, and green shoots will in time take over, if not removed.

For baskets, there are no better foliage plants. Start by placing cuttings directly into the basket potting soil.

Take care
Remove green growth.

Above: Tradescantia fluminensis 'Quicksilver' has bright silver variegation. It is best exhibited in hanging baskets.

Below: The superb bromeliad, Vriesea splendens, offers not only striking foliage but also a long-lasting 'sword' of red bracts.

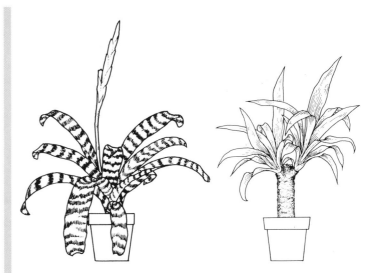

Vriesea splendens
(Flaming sword)

▶ **Good light; some sunshine**
▶ **Temp: 16-21°C (60-70°F)**
▶ **Keep moist; drier in winter**

This plant is a member of the bromeliad family with a typical rosette of overlapping leaves that form a natural urn for holding water. The urn must be kept topped up at all times but needs to be cleaned out and freshly watered every four to six weeks during the summer months.

The broad recurving leaves of *Vriesea splendens* are grey-green, with darker bands of brownish purple across the leaf. The flower spike usually develops in the summer and may last for many weeks. The bright red bracts enclosing the short-lived yellow flowers provide the main display.

Grow this plant in a mixture of equal parts loam-based growing medium and fir bark chips, or use a commercially prepared bromeliad mix. The main rosette flowers only once then dies, but as the plant deteriorates offsets form at the base of the trunk and, once rooted, these can be detached and potted separately.

Take care
Grow in bright light.

Yucca aloifolia
(Boundary plant, Dagger plant, Spanish bayonet)

▶ **Good light**
▶ **Temp: 10-21°C (50-70°F)**
▶ **Keep on the dry side**

The woody lengths of stem are imported from the tropics in very large quantities. They come in an assortment of sizes and are rooted at their destination, then potted and sold with their aloe-like tufts of growth at the top of the stem.

Further benefits of this plant are that they are pleasing to the eye when grouped together and little trouble to grow.

They do best in well-lit, coolish rooms if given the minimum of attention. The soil should be allowed to dry out quite appreciably between waterings and feed should be given once every 10 days during the summer.

Purchased plants are normally in pots relevant to their height, so the pot is often quite large. As a result, the plant is growing in a container in which it can remain for two years or more. Plants should be potted on only when they have filled their pots with roots. Use loam-based soil for this job.

Take care
Never overpot or overwater.

ove: Yucca aloifolia is a stately nt for a difficult location and it is y durable if not overwatered.

These plants are normally seen as stout stems with tufts of growth at the top.

INDEX OF COMMON NAMES

A
Action plant 35
African violet 40
Algerian ivy 28
Alpine violet 21
Aluminium plant 39
Amaryllis 30
Angels' wings 15
Aralia ivy 26
Asparagus fern 12
Assam rubber tree 27

B
Baby echeveria 24
Baby primrose 39
Barbados gooseberry 38
Barbados lily 30
Bar-room plant 12
Beef plant 33
Beefsteak plant 33
Benjamin tree 26
Bird's nest fern 13
Blacking plant 29
Blood leaf 33
Blushing bromeliad 36
Botanical-wonder tree 26
Boundary plant 45
Bowstring hemp 41
Brain plant 16
Brazilian gloxinia 43
Breadfruit vine 35
Button fern 37

C
Canary Island ivy 28
Cape cowslip 44
Cape primrose 44
Cartwheel plant 36
Cast iron plant 12
Cathedral windows 16
Chicken-gizzard 33
China rose 29
Chinese hibiscus 29
Christmas flower 25
Christmas star 25
Christ plant 25
Christ thorn 25
Cineraria 19
Claw cactus 42
Coral berry 11
Crab cactus 42
Croton 20
Crown of thorns 25

D
Dagger plant 45
Devil's ivy 42
Devil's tongue 41
Dudder grass 8
Dumb cane 22
Dutch hyacinth 32

E
Earth star 21
Easter cactus 40
Elephant's-ear 15
Elephant's-ear plant 9
Emerald feather 12
Emerald fern 12
Exotic brush 8

F
Fairy primrose 39
False aralia 11
Fancy-leaved caladium 15
Flaming Katy 34
Flamingo flower 10
Flaming sword 45
Florist's mum 18
Forster sentry palm 30
Freckle face 32
Fruit-salad plant 35

G
Golden English ivy 29
Golden evergreen 9
Golden pothos 42
Good luck palm 17
Good luck plant 41
Gloxinia 43

H
Heart-leaf philodendron 38
Hearts entangled 17
Hearts on a string 17
Hemp plant 41
Herringbone plant 34
Humble plant 35
Hurricane plant 35
Hyacinth 32

I
Indian azalea 13
India rubber tree 27
Iron cross begonia 14
Iron plant 12
Ivory pineapple 10
Ivy tree 26

JK
Java fig 26
Joseph's coat 20
Kangaroo vine 19
Kentia palm 30
King begonia 14

L
Lady's pocketbook 16
Lady's slippers 16
Leafy cactus 38
Lemon vine 38
Linkleaf 42
Little owl eyes 31

Little snakeskin plant 27
Live-and-Die 35
Lobster cactus 42
Lobster plant 25

M
Madagascar dragon tree 23
Madeira ivy 28
Maidenhair fern 8
Measles plant 32
Mexican breadfruit 35
Mexican flame leaf 25
Miniature wax plant 31
Mosaic plant 27
Mother-in-law plant 15
Mother-in-law's tongue 41
Mother-in-law's tongue plant 22

N
Nest fern 13
New Zealand cliffbrake 37

O
Orchid cactus 24
Owl eyes 31

P
Painted lady 24
Painted leaf 25
Painted-leaf begonia 14
Paper flower 15
Paradise palm 30
Parlour palm 17
Peace lily 43
Peacock plant 16
Pigtail plant 10
Pink cryptanthus 21
Pink dot plant 32
Pink jasmine 33
Pocketbook plant 16
Poinsettia 25
Polka dot plant 32
Pot chrysanthemum 18
Pouch flower 16
Prayer plant 34

R
Rainbow-star 21
Red pineapple 10
Rex begonia 14
Ribbon plant 18
Rosary vine 17
Rose of China 29
Rubber plant 27
Rugby football plant 37

S
St Bernard's lily 18
Screw pine 36
Sensitive plant 35

Sentry palm 30
Shame plant 35
Silk oak 28
Silky oak 28
Silver-net plant 27
Silver vase 8
Slipper flower 16
Slipperwort 16
Small-leaved rubber plant 26
Solomon Island ivy 42
Sowbread 21
Spanish bayonet 45
Spathe flower 43
Spiceberry 11
Spider ivy 18
Spider plant 18
Split-leaf philodendron 35
Spotted dieffenbachia 22
String of hearts 17
Striped dracaena 23
Sweetheart plant 38
Swiss cheese plant 35

T
Tailflower 10
Ten-commandments 34
Thanksgiving cactus 42
Thatch-leaf palm 30
Touch-me-not 35
Tree ivy 26
Tropic laurel 26
Tuftroot 22

U
Umbrella palm 22
Umbrella plant 22
Umbrella sedge 22
Umbrella tree 41
Urn plant 8

V
Variegated goldfish plant 20
Variegated laurel 20
Variegated parasol plant 41
Variegated silhouette plant 23
Vase plant 8
Veitch screw pine 36
Venus's-hair fern 8
Violet slipper gloxinia 43

W
Walking anthericum 18
Wandering Jew 44
Watermelon begonia 37
Watermelon peperomia 37
Watermelon pilea 39
Weeping fig 26
White flag 43
White sails 43
Window plant 35